The
Basket Book

The
Basket Book

by Don & Carol Raycraft

Photographs by Carol Raycraft

COLLECTOR BOOKS
P.O. Box 3009
Paducah, KY 42001

The current values in this book should be used only as a guide. They are not intended to set prices, which vary from one section of the country to another. Auction prices as well as dealer prices vary greatly and are affected by condition as well as demand. Neither the Author nor the Publisher assumes responsibility for any losses that might be incurred as a result of consulting this guide.

Acknowledgement

Mike and Martha Hilliard

Additional copies of this book may be ordered from:

COLLECTOR BOOKS
P.O. Box 3009
Paducah, Kentucky 42001

@$5.95 Add $1.00 for postage and handling.

Copyright: Don and Carol Raycraft, 1981
ISBN: 0-89145-174-9

Printed by IMAGE GRAPHICS, Paducah, Kentucky

Introduction

A standard comment that is delivered when somebody is struck by collector's lightning and decides to accumulate painted furniture or quilts is "It's too late." That means that the great cupboards in original paint or the Amish quilts have already been discovered and added to another collection. We have found that the statement is true to the extent that the vast majority of the "great" pieces are turning up less frequently and more expensively at shows and in shops and auction houses.

The rate at which textiles, furniture, Shaker, woodenware, baskets, decorated stoneware, and early lighting have been disappearing from the market place has been accentuated by the recent appearance of a variety of magazines and antiques oriented newspapers displaying homes furnished with country antiques.

A survey of books and magazines dealing with American antiques from the 1920's through the 1960's will seldom provide any insight into baskets or basket collecting for few were written about or offered for sale. American Indian baskets have been seriously collected for many years but mention of American country baskets did not appear with any degree of frequency until the early 1970's.

Collecting Baskets

Collectors who search for decorated stoneware pottery have learned to focus their attention on New York, Pennsylvania, Ohio, and New England because these are the areas where the early potteries were located. The potteries in the remainder of the nation were established at such a late date that very few pieces were still being elaborately decorated with cobalt slip.

The situation for basket collectors presents a different dilema because Indian and country basket makers were spread across the entire country during the nineteenth and early twentieth centuries, turning out a variety of basket forms. A search for a three gallon crock with a cobalt deer set in a wooded scene may be tough in Iowa or California but a short trip to a farm sale or a rural antiques shop in the same areas may turn up a rare basket form.

Baskets were designed to be used on a daily or seasonal basis. Berry baskets were used in the summer and spring and laundry baskets were used with each wash. When the bottom or sides of the baskets were damaged beyond reasonable repair, they were thrown away or used for kindling. They were not expensive nor difficult to acquire. They were functional in much the same manner as grocery bags are today. When a load of groceries arrives in our house, we often keep the bag for garbage or to carry out the ashes from the fireplace. If the bag is ripped or torn we throw it away. Nineteenth century homemakers treated splint baskets in a similar fashion.

That is precisely why handcrafted baskets in good condition are uncommon today and rare tomorrow.

Prices

When a collector of country antiques considers buying a basket, a primary ingredient of the selection process must be the condition of the basket. A piece of furniture can be restored or repaired to a minor degree without diminishing its value but a basket cannot. A basket with a portion of its bottom broken out or a handle snapped off is difficult to repair and much of the value is lost. A break in a piece of splint or a mouse hole in the bottom of a field basket is to be expected and does not hurt values. Country baskets were produced to be functional and many were in almost daily use. Wear and minor tears **should** be found on any old basket. A lifetime can be spent searching for a basket in perfect condition but it will be a fruitless trip if the mission is to locate an old basket and not a reproduction.

Basket prices tend to be more consistent across the nation than prices for stoneware or country furniture because baskets were produced in all areas and still may be found in use in many rural regions.

Sources

As indicated earlier, country baskets can be found almost anywhere. Perhaps, the single finest basket in our collection of over 200 was purchased in a "boutique" that sold polyester pants, plastic plants, and "antiques" in a rural community twenty minutes from our home.

It is also possible to spend a limited lifetime searching for baskets in small shops, at garage sales, and flea markets with mediocore success. The only advantage to this method is that when that great basket form is found it's probably going to be cheap.

There are numerous antiques publications (*Maine Antiques Digest, Ohio Antiques Review, Antiques and Arts Weekly*) which can provide insights into basket forms, current prices, dates and locations of major and minor shows and auctions, and hundreds of advertisements for dealers. We have purchased a number of baskets over the years through the mail from New England dealers. With each issue of these publications the number of uncommon basket forms presented dwindles. In 1975 a cheese basket was often available for $150.00 to $175.00. In 1981 the number of cheese baskets offered and the price asked for each are going in different directions. A collector today could easily expect to pay $350.00 to $550.00 for a cheese basket.

Our hunt has been slowed in recent years by the incredible demand and competition for country baskets. When collectors of Pier One baskets from the Phillipines see an article in *Country Living* or *House Beautiful* that features a home furnished with New England painted furniture, stoneware, and handcrafted early basket forms, a new world opens. Pier One loses many customers with each new article, the task for collectors becomes more difficult, and the price for the surviving baskets doubles.

Ladder-back side chair with splint seat of oak. The ball of splint (at left) and the seat of the chair are made of the same one quarter inch thick oak splint that was used in the construction of baskets. The ball of splint would have to be soaked in water until it was flexible enough to utilize in making baskets.

"Over two-under two" twill technique of making chair seats or baskets of splint.

Storage basket. Rib construction, oak splint, twisted hickory handle, 25" long x 16" high. $300.00-375.00.

Baskets in this form were often used for carrying rabbits, chickens, or other small fowl to market.

Close-up of twisted handle.

Market basket form. Rib construction, oak splint, twisted handles. $175.00-225.00,
$250.00-275.00

Close-up of "two strand" twisted handle.

Close-up of "three strand" twisted handle.

Field basket. 31" diameter, rib construction, oak splint, plaiting or checker-work weaving pattern, carved oak handles. $175.00-215.00.

Carved oak notched handles and "double wrapped" or "x-bound" rim of hickory splint.

Reinforced oak splint bottom of field basket.

Egg basket. Crudely made, oak splint, carved twig handle, possibly European in origin. Flat back allows basket to be hung on wall when not in use. $95.00-110.00.

Flat or wall back of egg basket.

Storage basket. Crudely made of oak splint, twig handle and pine "feet", possibly European in origin. $100.00-115.00.

Most "footed" baskets were designed for use in storing vegetables. The "feet" allowed air to circulate under the basket.

Farm or utility basket. 15" diameter, carved hickory handle, painted green on exterior and yellow on interior, possibly Shaker-made, found in New England. $200.00-250.00.

Field basket. Oval, 22" end to end, carved hickory handle, plaited weaving pattern, oak splint. $200.00-225.00.

Notched handle with tool marks. This handle is notched to fit between the inside and outside hoops of the double rim of the basket.

Storage basket. Oak splint, plaited or checkerwork construction, painted green, hickory splint wrapped rim. $95.00-115.00.

Garden basket. Used to gather flowers, herbs or vegetables. Oak splint, plaited construction,oak handle, early twentieth century, wrapped rim, iron nails holding handle to rim. $85.00-95.00.

Fruit drying basket. Pine frame, ash splint. The ribs of the drying basket are mortised into the frame and the sides are pinned. Apples were a critical part of the winter diet in the nineteenth century. They were picked in the fall, sliced, and allowed to dry on strings hung over the hearth or in the sun on drying racks or baskets of splints. $350.00-400.00.

Mortised frame of drying basket.

Apple picker's basket. Oak splint, New York state, late nineteenth century. $300.00-350.00.

"Kicked in" back of the apple picker's basket.

Field basket. 28" diameter, open plaited or checkerwork bottom, found in Illinois. $375.00-400.00.
The open weave bottom of the basket allowed accumulated dirt from produce to fall through and not add to the weight of the crop.

Shaker "2 pie" carrying basket. Ash splint cut on a veneering machine, copper rivets holding handle to the basket's side, early twentieth century. $200.00-250.00.

Handcrafted baskets are extremely difficult to date because a brief exposure to heavy use and the weather prematurely ages most works of splint. The problem of dating is further complicated by the consistency of basket forms over almost two centuries.

Shaker-made market basket. Machine cut swing handle, copper rivets, ash splint, late nineteenth-early twentieth century. $180.00-200.00.

Bottom of the Shaker market basket.

Shaker utility basket. Ash splint, New England, initialed by owner and dated (18) '63. $225.00-250.00.

The Shakers followed the lead of Indian craftsmen and used turned hardwood molds or forms to weave some baskets around. The form allowed the baskets to be tightly and consistently woven.

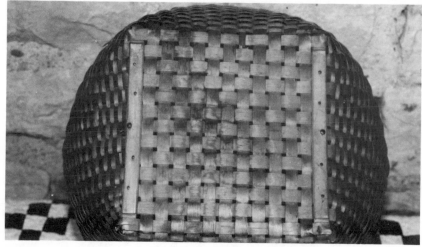

Checkerwork bottom with "runners" or "cleats". The runners were added to save tear and wear on the plaited basket bottoms.

Shaker woven poplar bureau boxes and doll bonnet, late nineteenth century, New England. Small box, $35.00-45.00; large box, $65.00-75.00; bonnet, $125.00-150.00.

Shaker trademark from Alfred, Maine community stamped on the bottom of the woven poplar bureau boxes.

Shaker miniature baskets. Ash splint, hickory handles, woven on a mold, late nineteenth century, produced for sale to the "world". $140.00-160.00; $150.00-175.00.

Checkerwork or plaited bottoms of miniature Shaker baskets.

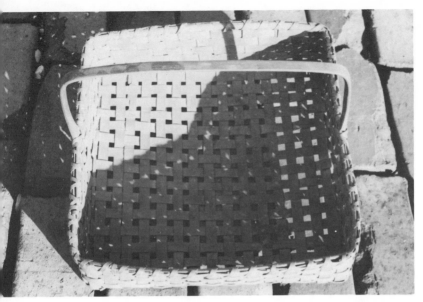

Herb tray, oak splint, early twentieth century, New England, x-bound rim wrapping. $125.00-140.00.

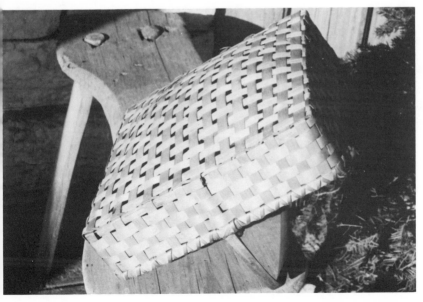

Checkerwork bottom of the herb tray.

Shaker carrier with seven berry baskets. 19" diameter, late nineteenth century. $300.00-375.00.

Individual wide splint berry baskets.

Rye straw, utility basket. Coil construction, hickory handle, 14" diameter.
$140.00-160.00
The individual coils of rye straw are bound with hickory splint. As the rye straw baskets age, the hickory binder begins to take on a darker patina.

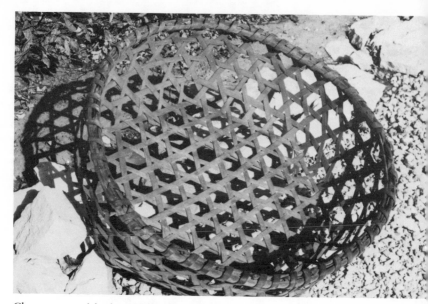

Cheese or curd basket. Hexagon weave, 26" diameter, New England, mid to late nineteenth century. $375.00-450.00.

Protective runners or cleats on the bottom of the cheese basket.

Unusually well made Shaker cheese or curd basket. 14" diameter, hexagon weave, oak splint. $450.00-550.00.

Interior of the cheese basket.

Swing or drop handle basket. Woven over a mold, ash splint, carved handle, rib construction, New England, late nineteenth century. $270.00-300.00.

Swing or drop handle basket. Oak splint, rib construction. The bottom of the basket is square and the top is round. Baskets used for a variety of purposes are referred to as utility baskets. $250.00-300.00.

Carved steeple or bow, notched and inserted between the double rims and held by weavers to the side of the basket.

Swing or drop handle basket. Ash splint, double wrapped rim, New England, 14
diameter. $225.00-250.00.

Swing or drop handle basket. Painted blue, unusually spread handle bows or steeple
found in New Hampshire, mid-nineteenth century. $350.00-400.00.

Turned pine basket bottom. Cut iron nails, uncommon form.

Shaker feather-type basket. Woven around a mold, slotted or slide cover, ash splint, New England. $150.00-165.00.

Shaker, feather-type basket. Slide cover or top. Tightly woven over a mold, painted green, New England, ash splint, nineteenth century. $250.00-275.00.

Bulbous bottom of feather basket.

Shaker feather-type basket. Woven over mold, ash splint, New England. $200.00-225.00.

Sewing or "work" basket. Rib construction, "kicked in" or "demi-john" bottom, double wrapped rim, hickory handles. $125.00-140.00.

Nantucket "lightship" basket. Rib construction, woven on a mold, turned pine bottom, swing or drop handle, imported rattan (cane) weavers, probably early twentieth century. $350.00-400.00.

Baskets of this type were first made on the South Shoal Lightship off the coast of Nantucket, Massachusetts in the mid-nineteenth century. The baskets were initially made in nests of 5 and 8. In the early 1900's several makers turned out nests of 7 baskets. Nantucket baskets are distinguished by the use of rattan that was carried back to the island by American sailors from ports in the Phillipine Islands, China, and India. The wooden bottoms were turned on the island and added to the basket aboard the lightship.

Turned pine bottom of Nantucket basket.

Bottom of Shaker-made basket from Maine. A basket with a "kicked-in" or a turned wooden bottom was designed to carry loads that could endanger the health of baskets like this example. The wide ash splint was woven tightly over a mold.

Algonkian or Iroquois utility basket. 7" long x 5" wide, x 4" high, checkerwork pattern, colored weavers, late nineteenth century. The value of a basket can be increased if the weavers carry decoration or good color. It is not uncommon to find a basket with weavers that are freshly dyed, painted, or stained to enhance the value of the basket. $75.00-85.00.

"Potato"-type stamped basket. Red and blue stamps, heart on each side, 14" long x 12" wide x 6½" high, New England, mid-nineteenth century, black ash splint, checker work construction, probably Algonkian Indian. $115.00-130.00.

Knife and fork basket. Oak splint, carved bow type handle, painted green, late nineteenth century, 11" long x 6½" wide x 5" high. $140.00-175.00.

Bobbin or comb basket. Indian made, painted green, New England, late nineteenth century. A comb basket was hung on a wall with a small mirror propped against the back and toilet articles could be stored inside. A bobbin is a wooden cylinder or spindle on which yarn or thread is wound. The basket was on a loom post and bobbins were stored in the basket. $125.00-150.00.

Miniature melon basket. Ash splint, found in Pennsylvania, 5½" across, rib construction, hickory splint handle. $115.00-145.00.

Buttocks basket. Rib construction, 11" diameter, exceptionally well made, late nineteenth century. $175.00-200.00.

Egg basket. Buttocks form, rib construction, oak splint, late nineteenth century. $175.00-200.00.

Buttocks egg basket. Oak splint, double thick splint handle, 9½'' diameter x 7½'' high. $120.00-135.00.

Unusually oversized buttocks basket. Triple thick hickory splint handle, oak splint, rib construction, 20½" diameter x 18" high. $250.00-275.00.

Utility basket. Ash splint, woven over a mold, Shaker-made, New England, late nine-teenth century. $110.00-120.00.

Interior of tightly woven Shaker basket.

Market basket. Oak splint, checker weave, late nineteenth-early twentieth century
$110.00-125.00.

Notched handle of market basket.

Indian-made basket. Carved handles, curlicue or "curly" ribbon decoration, ash splint, probably late nineteenth century. $100.00-140.00.

Checkerwork interior of curlicue basket.

Footed storage or drying basket. 30" x 14" x 12", early nineteenth century, mortise and tenon construction of the frame. $400.00-475.00.

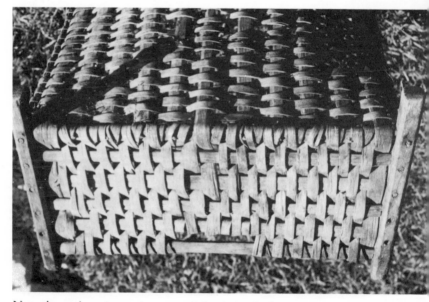

Note the tool marks on the posts of the drying basket.

Winnowing basket. Oak splint, wide pine hoop, carved hickory handles, mid to late nineteenth century. $375.00-450.00.

Handle of winnowing basket lashed with splint to the pine hoop or rim.

Over lap of the hoop of the winnowing basket.

Classic field basket. New England, mid-nineteenth century, 32" across x 16" high. $300.00-350.00.

Field or garden basket. Unusual braided handle, rib construction, oak splint, late nineteenth century, 32" x 18" x 13". $275.00-300.00.

Storage or utility basket. Tighty woven on a mold, ash splint, carved oak bows, rib construction, late nineteenth century, 13" diameter. $140.00-160.00.

Storage basket for table use with fruits or vegetables. Splayed sides, Indian-made, alternating dyed weavers, bow handles, checkerwork bottom. $80.00-95.00.

The manner in which this basket is constructed is a hint of its purpose. The small handles could support little weight and are more decorative than functional.

Rear view of fruit or vegetable storage basket.

Table or storage basket. Rectangular base and oval mouth or top, painted green, oak splint, double rim, late nineteenth century. $100.00-115.00.

Checkerwork bottom of the storage basket.

Open weave gathering or charcoal basket. Oak splint, carved notched handles. $135.00-150.00.

Open weave checkerwork bottom.

Storage basket with open weave bottom. Hickory handles, 14" x 10" x 5½". $150.00-165.00.

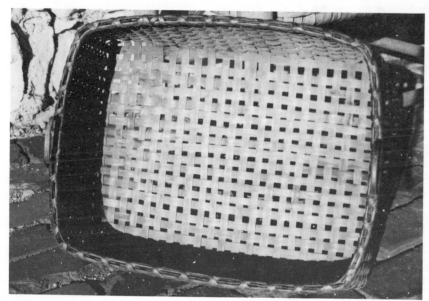

Close-up of open weave bottom.

Wall Baskets

The next four baskets illustrated are similar in their weaving patterns and rib construction. In the southern United States, half baskets are often described as "key" baskets. They were used to hold keys to storage areas or out buildings.

Half basket. $145.00-175.00.

Half basket. $100.00-125.00.

Half basket. $100.00-125.00.

Half basket. $90.00-115.00.

Miniature basket. Carved handle, painted orange with black decorations, tightly woven oak splint, double rim, mid-nineteenth century. $350.00-425.00.

Ash splint cradle. Pine floor, oak rims, cut iron nails, traces of old red stain, early nineteenth century, 41" x 16", New England. $650.00-800.00.

Interior of the cradle, pine floor and molding.

Glossary of Basket Terms

Buttocks basket - A form that allows relatively heavy or delicate loads to be evenly distributed in a basket without breaking or falling through the bottom.

Checker work - A standard technique in weaving baskets of "one over-one under-one over" repeatedly. Also called plain plaiting.

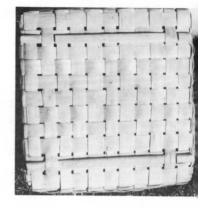

Cheese weave - A hexagonal weaving pattern often used in making cheese, curd, or finely woven drying baskets.

Half basket - Exactly what the name implies. In the southern U.S. the half basket was usually called a "key" basket and hung on a wall for storage of keys to out buildings or storage cupboards.

"Kicked in" bottom - A "kicked in", "kicked up", or "demi-john" bottom allowed the basket's contents to be distributed away from the center of the basket.

Notched handles - The basket handles or bows were usually carved from oak or hickory and inserted through the double rim and held by weavers to the sides of the basket. The carved notch and the outside rim provided a tight fit and security.

Open work - The open weave checker work allowed water, mud, and sand to easily fall through the bottom of the basket.

"Potato" stamp decoration - A decorative technique used primarily by eastern Indian tribes on wide splint baskets. A raised design was carved on a turnip, potato, or piece of soft wood and dipped into color produced by juices and stains from plants and berries. The process may also be described as block stamping and was used until the early 1900's.

Rim - A basket may have a single or double rim. A rim was made from a hoop of oak or hickory splint and bound to the basket through several techniques. The splint wrapped around the rim in this example and can be described as double wrapped, cross-bound, x-bound, or double bound.

Runners - Strips of thick splint added as a protective buffer between the bottom of the basket and the ground. May also be called "cleats" or "heels" in some areas.

Rye straw - A type of basket woven with coils of rye straw bound with hickory splint. Rye straw baskets may also be called "beehive" baskets. The example shown is also called a "dough basket".

Signed - A basket that is signed carries its maker's signature in pencil, ink, or is burned into the splint. Signed baskets are not frequently encountered. This Shaker example has the initials of the probable owner and the date (18) '63.

Slide lid - Type of lid, top, or basket cover found on feather baskets. The slide lid is fixed permanently to the handle in such a manner that it is slid up and down to put things in or take things out of the basket.

Splint - Narrow, usually flat strips of ash, oak, hickory or other wood used in weaving baskets or chair seats. May be called "split" in some areas.

Swing handle - A swing or drop handle is a carved piece of hickory or oak splint attached to the bows in such a manner that it can move freely. The opposite is a fixed handle.

Twill - A weaving pattern similar to plaiting but done "under two-over two-under two" or in a similar variation.

Veneering machine - A machine that precisely and quickly sliced thin strips of wood. This procedure suddenly put makers of handcrafted splint baskets out of business. Baskets made from machine cut splint became popular in the mid-1880's. They tend to be made with splints similar to those in the basket pictured.

Wash basket - May also be referred to as a laundry basket. This example might even be called a field basket.

Wicker - Rods or twigs from the willow tree used in the construction of baskets or furniture. Some authorities define wicker as willow with the bark peeled or removed from the rods or twigs.

Work basket - A tightly woven, round, splint basket with bow handles. Work baskets tend to have a larger diameter than height and a "demi-john" bottom. Work baskets were used often to hold sewing materials and projects.

Study Guide

The following questions are offered to test your knowledge of the text and pictures.

1. The bottom of this basket

    a. has been plaited.
    b. is woven with a checker work pattern.
    c. could be described as "open work".
    d. all of the above.
    e. none of the above.

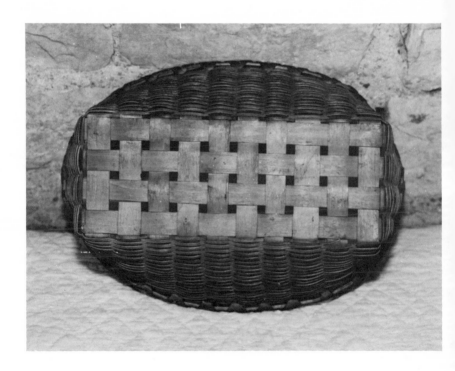

2. A close look at this basket shows

True   False   x-bound wrapping.
True   False   a double rim.
True   False   drop handles.

3. True   False   This is a cheese basket.

4. True   False   This is a hexagon weave basket.

5. This basket **has**

    True   False   a double wrapped rim.
    True   False   rib construction.
    True   False   been made of rye straw splint lashed with hickory splint.
    True   False   a twill weave.

6. True   False   This is an example of coiled construction.

Study Guide Answers

1. d

2. True
   True
   False

3. False - This is a drying basket.

4. True - This is a basket with a cheese or hexagon weave.

5. False
   True
   False
   False

6. False

Suggested Reading List

There are not a great many basket books currently in print that are worth your time if they are competing with a syndicated adventure of James Rockford and Angel Martin in the "Rockford Files".

We recommend the following books and have added a few editorial remarks.

1. Gould, Mary Earle, *Early American Woodenware*, Charles E. Tuttle and Co., 1962.

    Even though there is not a wealth of material in this book dealing with baskets, we always recommend it because is is our favorite book on antiques. We had the chance to meet Miss Gould and enjoyed her as much as her books.

2. Larason, Lew, *The Basket Collector's Book*, Science Press, undated.

3. Lasansky, Jeannette, *Willow, Oak, and Rye: Basket Traditions in Pennsylvania*, 1978.

4. Raycraft, Don and Carol, *Country Baskets*, Wallace-Homestead, 1976.
    The only book done to date with full color pictures.

5. Seeler, Katherine and Edgar, *Nantucket Lightship Baskets*, Deermouse Press, 1972.

    This is a superior basket book that is very hard to find. It is the definitive book dealing with the baskets of Nantucket.

6. Teleki, Gloria Roth, *The Baskets of Rural America*, Dalton, 1975.

7. Teleki, Gloria Roth, *Collecting Traditional American Basketry*, Dutton, 1979.

    Both Mrs. Teleki's books are well written and contain carefully selected pictures. The 1975 volume is superior in our opinion, to the 1979 book, and is a "must" for basket collectors to add to their libraries. She puts a great deal of emphasis on newly made baskets and Indian baskets.

Basket Inventory

As the price of baskets escalate and the quantity diminishes, it may be necessary to keep an accurate record of the sources and prices of the baskets in your collection. The replacement costs for insurance purposes often are not believed by insurance agents and if you are like us you have already lost the receipts. To meet a variety of needs we provide you with a place to keep track of the additions to your growing basket collection.

	Type of Basket	Approx. Age	Purchased Where?	Purchased From Whom?	When?	Price Paid?
1.						
2.						
3.						
4.						
5.						
6.						
7.						
8.						
9.						
10.						
11.						
12.						
13.						
14.						
15.						
16.						
17.						

	Type of Basket	Approx. Age	Where?	Purchased From Whom?	When?	Price Paid?
18.						
19.						
20.						
21.						
22.						
23.						
24.						
25.						
26.						
27.						
28.						
29.						
30.						
31.						
32.						
33.						
34.						
35.						
36.						
37.						
38.						
39.						

Dealer Directory

	Name of Shop	Address	Telephone Number	Dealer's Name	Type of Merchandise
1.					
2.					
3.					
4.					
5.					
6.					
7.					
8.					
9.					
10.					
11.					
12.					
13.					
14.					
15.					
16.					
17.					
18.					
19.					
20.					
21.					